BORN TO
OVERCOME
DR. D. K. OLUKOYA

Dr. D.K. Olukoya

ISBN: 978-0692388082

A Publication of
TRACTS AND PUBLICATIONS GROUP
MOUNTAIN OF FIRE AND MIRACLES MINISTRIES
13, Olasimbo Street, off Olumo Road,
(By UNILAG Second Gate), Onike, Iwaya.
P.O.Box 2990, Sabo, Yaba, Lagos, Nigeria.
08023308127, 01-7747198, 01-7303485
Website: www.mountainoffire.org
E-mail: mfmhqworldwide@mountainoffire.org

I salute my wonderful wife, Pastor Shade, for her invaluable support in the ministry. I appreciate her unquantifiable support in the book ministry as the cover designer, art editor, and art advisor.

First Edition

TABLE OF CONTENTS

INTRODUCTION

This book focuses on the principles of overcoming and the secrets of greatness.

Deuteronomy 28:13 says, "**And the Lord shall make thee the head, and not the tail; and thou shall be above only. And thou shall not be beneath; if that thou hearken unto the commandments of the Lord thy God, which I command thee this day, to observe and to do them.**"

The agenda of the Almighty is that all His children should be overcomers.

John 16:33 says, "**These things I have spoken unto you, that in me ye might have peace. In the world, ye shall have tribulations. But be of good cheer; I have overcome the world.**"

FACTS ABOUT OVERCOMING

1. It is emergencies that make or produce giant men. Goliath was an emergency and when David showed up, the emergency made David a giant killer.

2. It is the rough seas and storms that make good sailors. You cannot claim to be a real pilot or captain, when you have not faced turbulent seas or situations.

3. It is wars that make generals. And without adversity, you will never know the kind of materials you are made of.

4. The same sun that melts the wax also hardens the clay. The same trouble that some people face and they collapse will strengthen others.

5. For a Christian, every adversity is usually a blessing in disguise.

6. Every failure will teach you a lesson and that you will need to learn. Proverbs 24:10 says, "**If thou faint in the day of adversity, thy strength is small.**"

7. When your spiritual temperature is high enough, it will kill all internal demons. It is only a mad fly or mosquito that can perch on a hot electric iron.

8. A man is not a sinner because he is a drunkard but he is a drunkard because he is a sinner. Sin is a disaster to everyone who wants to overcome.

9. If television is the lord of your evening, do not expect divine visitation or night vision because you are probably going to carry into your vision what you have been watching.

10. If you try to please everybody, you are a student

in the school of failure; that is, if you try to be everything to everybody, you will end up being nothing to everybody.

11. All men must stumble often before they reach the top. Only a worm is free from worry and stumbling.

Fighters do not give up in a hurry. They see life as a challenge and their desire is to make it. They see life as a duty and want to perform it. They see life as an opportunity and they want to take it. They see life as a journey and they want to complete it.

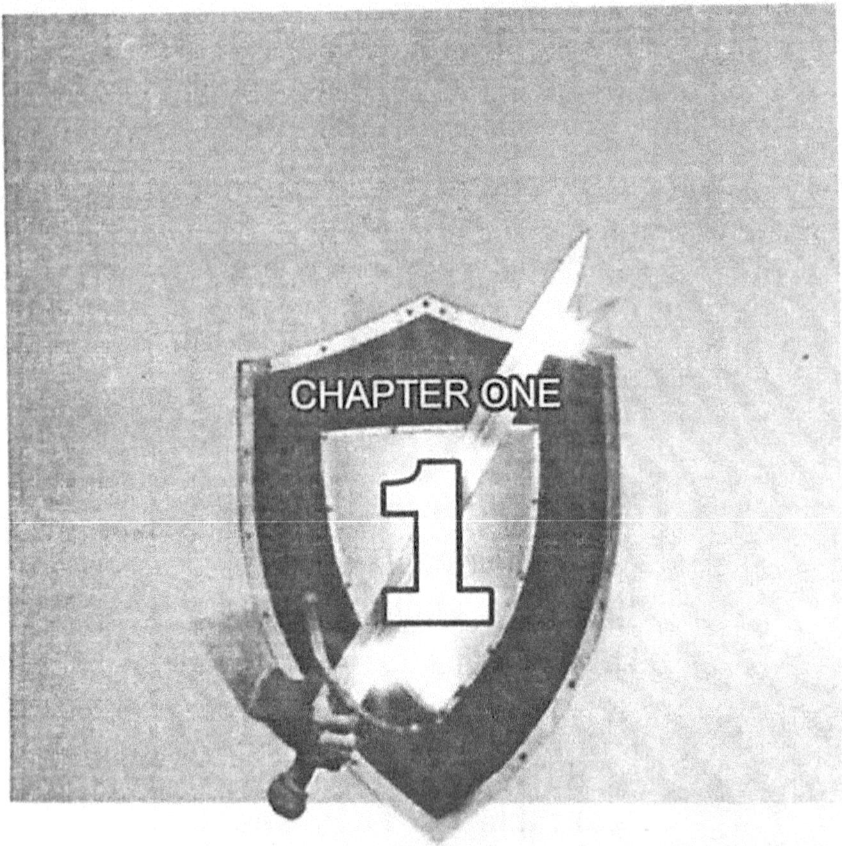

INSTRUCTIONS TO THOSE WHO WANT TO OVERCOME

1. **You must have the fighting spirit:** The Bible says, "Fight the good fight of faith" (1 Timothy 6: 12). It also says, "**From the days of John the Baptist until now; the kingdom of God suffereth violence, and the violent taketh it by force"** (Matthew 11: 12).

Many times we are too passive for God to do anything. Often times, we allow the status quo to just go on without the desire and action for a meaningful change. Anytime our expectations are not met or we do not get something right, we have a tendency to collapse or give up. Such an attitude annoys heaven. The reason we read about Jacob in the Bible today is that he was a fighter.

He knew that he was not in the position of blessing and if he continued that way, he would die a wretched man. He fought his way out until the angel of God blessed him. The reason we are also reading about blind Bartimaeus is that he was a fighter. Unfortunately, we have a new generation of Christians whose only objective is to occupy conquered territories. They are only looking for comfort zones, which is very sad. The Bible regards the house of God as a military barracks; a place where you fight. That is why these days, you see some young men, who are looking for women who already have flats and cars to marry so that they will do nothing.

That is laziness, and I consider such young men to be strange. You also notice another category of young men who should rather sit down and do their carpentry, tailoring, or building work but they would say, "I want to be a pastor, for God has called me."

This is contrary to the Scriptures because the people God calls are those who are very busy doing their work. They do not even want to leave their work to serve God. But nowadays, you see some people carrying suitcases with stickers on them and claiming to be pastors. At this juncture, I would like you to declare this loud and clear: "O God, arise and give me the fighting spirit, in the name of Jesus."

Fighters do not give up in a hurry. They see life as a challenge and their desire is to make it. They see life as a duty and want to perform it. They see life as an opportunity and they want to take it. They see life as a journey and they want to complete it. They see life as a promise and want to fulfil it. They see life as a field and want to cultivate it. They see life as a struggle and want to fight it.

I know a sister who comes from a humble background. She struggled and got her first degree and struggled and got a Masters degree. Thereafter, she had no job for five years. One day, she attended a service; where the preacher quoted the Scriptures which say that the violent takes it by force and she got angry within her and began a seven-day dry fast. On the seventh day, she saw her credentials buried in a pit. As she continued the prayers, she saw an angel of God walk to the place, opened the pit, brought out her credentials and handed them over to her. The following day, she got invitation from four companies to attend four interviews and the day after that, three out of the four companies gave her appointment letters. Then she was left with the headache of choice. If she had sat down and crossed her legs waiting for 'God's time' or said, "What's gonna be; is gonna be," she would have remained jobless. She fought and got her breakthrough.

Born to overcome could mean born to fight because you do not overcome until you have confronted and conquered the enemy. You can only overcome through a battle.

Born to overcome is equal to born to fight because there can be no winners without fighters. It does not matter your circumstances. You can start small and grow from there. Many people pray but they do not possess the raw materials for God to work on. In spite of the hard situation that we complain about, there are still people who are making it.

2. Form good habits and become a slave to them: Romans 6:16 says, **"Know ye not that to whom ye yield yourselves servants to obey, his servants ye are to whom you obey: whether of sin unto death, or of obedience unto righteousness."**

All men are slaves to their habits. Bad habits can imprison your future so, they must be destroyed. If you must overcome all the time, you must first of all become a slave to good habits. Habits are acts which become easy through constant repetition. Do not embrace negative habits such as lateness, eating all the time, prayerlessness, talkativeness and gossiping because they will make you to fail in life.

3. You must have the love of God in your heart: I Corinthians 13:8 says, **"Charity never faileth; but whether there be prophecies, they shall fail; whether there be tongues, they shall cease;**

whether there be knowledge, it shall vanish away."

Love is the greatest secret of success in all ventures. Muscles can destroy lives but only the unseen power of love can melt the heart of men. You must love all manner of men for they all have their own qualities to be admired. People with the love of God in their hearts do not look for excuses to gossip, and they are always themselves. They would particularly check anything that enters into their bodies, souls and spirits. You must have this quality as a Christian. Jesus said, "By this shall men know that you are my disciples if you l Love one another."

4. You must persist until you succeed: You should not give up in a hurry. Proverbs 24:16 says, **"For a just man falleth seven times, and riseth up again but the wicked shall fall into mischief."**

You must know for sure that God did not bring you into this world to be a failure. Failure does not run in your blood. God wants you to be an eagle. So, you must refuse to talk, walk and sleep with chickens. God has not created a failure and if God is your Father, it therefore means that your surname is God and as a child of God, you must not fail.

5. You must see your uniqueness: I Peter 2:9 says, **"But ye are a chosen generation, a royal priesthood, an holy nation, a peculiar people; that ye should show forth the praises of him who hath called you out of darkness into his marvellous light."**

You must realize that God created only one of you. None came before you, there is none living now, and none will come tomorrow. No one can be exactly like you. Every human being is a unique creature. But if you do not use your God-given potentials, you will be stagnant. Nobody came to this world by chance that is why you must constantly seek to know and to do what God wants you to do.

6. You must refuse to live in yesterday: Philippians 3:13 says, **"Brethren, I count not myself to have apprehended; but this one thing I do, forgetting those things which are behind, and reaching forth unto those things which are before."**

You must refuse to live in yesterday. Do not waste your precious time mourning yesterday's defeat, misfortune or failure. You cannot become younger than yesterday because it is buried for ever. A wasted day is a destruction of a page in the book of one's life. You must avoid the powers that kill time and return you to where you are not supposed to be.

7. Master your emotions: Proverbs 15: 32 says, **"He that is slow to anger is better than the mighty; and he that ruleth his spirit than he that taketh a city."**

You are a weak person when your emotions control your actions. Do not allow the forces of darkness to capture you using your emotions. You must depart from the school of anger, malice, envy, hatred, self-pity and lust. You must master your mood. When your enemies control your life, you are already a failure.

8. You must have a goal in life: I Corinthians 9:26 says, **"I therefore so run, not as uncertainly; so fight I, not as one that beateth the air."**

You must have a goal. A corn of wheat has three functions: to be fed to the swine, to be ground for bread or to be planted to multiply. You should not allow your life to be fed to the swine. You should not allow the rod of failure to ground your life. You must set goals for the day, week, month and year. Consider your best performance of the past and decide to multiply it to higher standards.

Somebody said, "It is better to aim your arrow at the moon and strike an eagle than to aim at the eagle and strike the rock." You must decide to climb higher than you are today. Do not commit the terrible crime of aiming low. You must have a goal so that you can focus and know where you are going.

9. You must be a reader: This is one area, where we have serious trouble especially in this part of the world. Books are part of the most important agents of impartation. Books are very powerful and God's people have written and published so many. The tragedy of this generation is that they do not read books. They prefer to go to the internet, play computer games and do all sorts of frivolous things. Many believers do not even read any book except prayer books. This generation is that of non-readers and is basically 'bookblind.' What reading can do for you, laying on of hands, prayer and fasting cannot do it for you.

Sometimes, laying on of hands, prayer and fasting instead of reading, is like eating groundnut in order to quench your thirst. Books can teach you so many things. Books can open your mind. Books can give you a ministry. Books can make you understand God better. Books can lead you into a divine encounter. One glance at a book can make you hear the voice of an author who died a thousand years ago. That is why they say, "Show me the book a man reads and I will know the man." If you want to destroy a culture, you need not burn the books but get the people to stop reading the books.

Books are masters. They instruct us without beating. They tell us words without getting angry.

They teach us without bread or money. Books do not fall asleep like our teacher sometimes would. If you seek them, you will find them. They do not hide like teachers sometimes do. If you make a blunder, the book will not laugh at you. If you are ignorant, it will not scold you. The advantage of books over oral instructions is that they are willing to repeat their instructions over and over again.

Daniel 9:2 says, **"In the first year of his reign I**

Daniel understood by books the number of the years, whereof the word of the Lord come to Jeremiah, the prophet, that he would accomplish seventy years in the desolations of Jerusalem."

Through books, Daniel understood things. Paul requested that his books be brought to him while he was in prison. Books are a collection of writers' thoughts, and through them, you know what to do with your life. You have to do something about your reading habit if you must be an overcomer. You must drop the addiction to television, internet, movies, useless discussions and gossips.

Reading is not a gift but a choice. You must read at least one book in two weeks. This is a very serious matter. I want you to understand it and build a small library for yourself. Books are treasures much more than clothes, houses and cars. What you hear may go away but what you read stays. A non-reading person is a closed person.

10. Soak your life in prayer.

11. Soak yourself in the word of God. As you follow up these instructions, the spirit of the over- comer will come upon your life.

PRAYER POINTS

1. My hidden treasures buried in secret, come out now, in the name of Jesus.
2. My mouth, receive the anointing of the over-comer, in the name of Jesus.
3. Evil load of my father's house assigned to arrest my destiny, die, in the name of Jesus.
4. Every virtue, every blessing and every breakthrough, that I have lost, I recover them by fire, in the name of Jesus.
5. Embargo power assigned to stop me; you are a liar, die, in the name of Jesus.
6. Every distance that I have lost, I repossess them in the name of Jesus.
7. Power of Pharaoh of my father's house, what are you waiting for? Die, in the name of Jesus.

The man who despises
what he has now
because he feels it is
not much will lose even
what he has.
If you want to be
great, then become
diligent with the little
that you have now.

CHAPTER TWO

2

BIBLICAL SECRETS OF GREATNESS

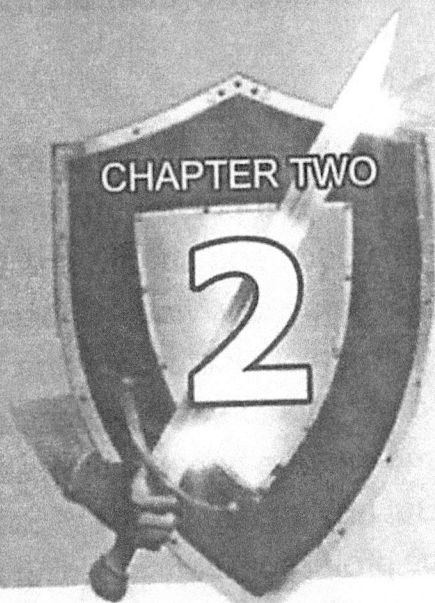

Psalm 71:21 says, "Thou shall increase my greatness and comfort me on every side."

A certain Nigerian lady doctor graduated and sought employment abroad. She prayed the kind of prayers you will find in this book and shortly, she got the job. Her score at the interview was 75 per cent. She became the most junior doctor working in that big hospital. The other doctors were consultants and professors. Some of them became professors before she was born. But anytime the cases of patients were reviewed and the professors concluded on what to do, the lady would say, "Excuse me sirs, it will not work, this is what will work." She would then give her own recommendation. The professors would tell her that they were more knowledgeable than her so she should keep quiet. But at the end of the day, they would adopt her suggestion and it worked 100 per cent every time. So, she became popular in the hospital, and everyone wanted to see her. The Lord increased her greatness in that place and nobody could sack her. She became an asset to that hospital. That is what happens when you do some things and pray some prayers as you would find in this book.

WHAT DOES GREATNESS MEAN?

Greatness means to be larger in size, quality or number than others of the same kind. It means to be remarkable or to have an outstanding performance in what you are doing. It means to be superior in quality. It means to be powerful. It means to become a man or woman of influence. It means to have a distinguished personality or to be glorious. God has created men and women to be great. the question is, how many fulfill this destiny?

FACTS ABOUT GREATNESS

Let us examine some facts about greatness according to the word of God.

1. Your present is the key to your future. You use what

you have now to get what you will use in future. Your present is the seed for that which you would become in future.

2. Greatness does not usually begin great. So, if you despise your little beginning, you will never be great. Jesus taught His disciples that the way to become a master is to become the servant of all.

   Mark 10:43-44 says, **"But so shall it not be among you: but whosoever will be great among you, shall be your minister. And whosoever of you will be the chiefest, shall be servant of all."**

It is the principle of greatness. A small person who is diligent will never remain small but will sooner or later become great. Many people want to start from the top but it never works that way, you start from the bottom and God will lift you up. The Bible makes us to understand that the way up is down.

Luke 16:10 says, **"He that is faithful in that which is least is faithful also in much: and he that is unjust in the least is unjust also in much."**

Verse 12: **"And if ye have not been faithful in that which is another man's, who shall give you that which is your own?"**

God will not give you your own, if you do not prove yourself reliable when serving others. The way you serve others will show whether you will become great or not. Some people who are lazy would say, "I am only here for a while, I have not started. When I start, I will not be lazy." That is not the principle of greatness. The way you work when you are working for somebody is the way the anointing of greatness will come upon you. When you ask some pastors, who are working under a General Overseer to go on three days vigil, they would say, "No, you want to kill me? You do not want me to stay with my family." But when they go out to start their own churches, they will declare forty days vigil, which they refused to do when they were working under somebody. Such pastors will never be great.

When you are working for somebody and you are busy stealing money and wrecking the place, you are a glorified rat in that company. When you start your own company, someone else will become a giant rat there, because that was what you did when you were working under somebody else. Sometimes, God makes a person an apprentice under somebody before he becomes a master of himself. Your period of apprenticeship is the gate way of your future. You will never increase if you reject or despise your little starting point. The seed of your future is in your present. Your future greatness is in the little you have now. And no matter how big a door is, you need a little key to open it. You should understand this principle.

When God gives you five talents, He is really telling

you that your proper place is among those with ten talents. God will not start you off with seven talents when He knows that, that is your limit. No, He will give you three and expect you to use them to find the other four. That way, you would become better equipped to manage the extra.

The man who despises what he has now because he feels it is not much will lose even what he has. If you want to be great, then become diligent with the little that you have now. If you want to be your own master in the future, then become a faithful servant to your masters now.

Proverbs 18:16 says, **"A man's gift maketh room for him, and bringeth him before great men."**

3. Another secret of greatness is that in every life, there is a deposit of greatness. There is something God has deposited in you to make you great. That is why someone said that the

greatest treasure ground; the richest place on earth is the cemetery, because in the cemetery, there are dead visions, dead dreams, dead ideas, dead talents, dead knowledge, dead brains, imaginations etc. God has deposited something in you to bring you to greatness, but that thing can be stolen, destroyed, ignored, abused, perverted, suffocated, wasted, exchanged or transferred. This is where prayer comes in.

There are many people whose greatness have been stolen, wasted or ignored. For Joseph in the Bible, the deposit of greatness that God put in his life was the gift of dreams. Ironically, it was this gift that put him in trouble. But eventually, it was the same gift that promoted him from prison to the palace, meaning that your key to greatness can change the course of your life through a crisis before you get to glory.

Rahab, the prostitute in the Bible had the deposit of hospitality in her life. One day, she was hospitable to some people and her life changed. She was rooted in evil but her hospitality made her to be uprooted from evil and to be rooted in Jesus Christ.

Daniel had the deposit of effectual fervent prayers in the face of all kinds of adversities and that catapulted him to greatness. For Samson, it was his strength but unfortunately, he abused it. What brought David to limelight was his ability to play music. That was what brought him to the palace of the king. The art of fishing exposed Peter to limelight. You need to know the key of greatness deposited in your destiny, so that you do not begin to use another person's own. You need to pray to identify your key to greatness.

Deal with your foundation, address your root problem. If you do not deal with them, they will pull you down.

KEYS TO GREATNESS

Let us consider the keys to greatness:

1. Find God. When you find God, other things will follow. The Bible says, "And ye shall seek me and find me, when ye shall search for me with all your heart" (Jeremiah 29:13). When you make God the head, there will be progress.

2. Ensure that you marry the right person. This one decision will determine 90 per cent of your success. If you miss God's will for your life in marriage, you miss a lot.

3. Be forgiving.

4. Be generous. Do not be stingy; the stingy man will die in his stinginess.

5. Have a grateful heart. Learn to say, 'Thank you.'

6. Never give up, be persistent.

7. Treat everyone you meet the way you want

yourself or children to be treated.

8. Commit yourself to constant improvement.

9. Commit yourself to excellence and quality.

10. Be loyal to the authority under which you are serving.

11. Be honest always. Tell the truth.

12. Be prayerful.

13. Be holy.

14. Be a Bible addict.

15. Deal with your foundation, address your root problem. If you do not deal with them, they will pull you down.

A certain woman had six boys and kept saying that she wanted a girl. And because of that, she got pregnant the seventh time but the seventh one was a boy too.

Everyday, she would be telling the boy that he was supposed to have come as a girl and that as far as she was concerned, he was a girl. Indeed, that was what followed him throughout his life before he started praying. He was a man in a woman's clothing and everything he had was negative until he came for prayers. Immediately he prayed the first prayer point, a strange voice spoke through him saying, "Please, leave him alone, he is a woman. Why do you want him to become a man? It can never be." Until that foundation was dealt with, that man never became great.

Sometime ago, a couple had two beautiful daughters, and because they were very beautiful, they went to a herbalist who prepared charms for them so that they would not be impregnated in school. As a result, men did not come or talk to them.

They were always going their way. One became an Accountant and the other a Medical Doctor. At ages 42 and 40, they were not married and no man came to them. Unfortunately for them, their parents died and nobody could tell them what happened until they came for prayers. After some serious prayers, one of their uncles who was still alive told them the truth about what their father did and said they should pray that the herbalist who did it was still alive in the village. Their uncle went in search of the herbalist. He got him and reminded him about their case. He told the herbalist that the girls needed to marry. The herbalist told him to go back home, and under their father's bed, he would find a bottle placed upside down; he should turn it up and they would be okay. That was what he did and the ladies became free. The bottle had two carved images inside it. The problem of the root was preventing them from being great.

At this juncture, I would like you to make the following confession aggressively. The way you do it will determine the level of your breakthrough:

"*The Almighty God, the God of Abraham, Isaac and*

Jacob will over-answer my prayers for breakthrough, in the name of Jesus. By the bulldozing power of the Holy Spirit, all obstacles on my way of greatness shall die, in Jesus' name. Whether it is convenient for the enemy or not, God shall be God in my situation, in Jesus' name. If I have placed my hands on a programme of failure, I take my hands off by fire, in the name of Jesus.

The vulture of my father's house and my mother's house designed to feed on the carcass of my destiny shall die, in the name of Jesus. Every move of my enemy shall bring me testimony, in the name of Jesus. The oil of greatness assigned for my head will not run dry, in the name of Jesus.

Any pattern of darkness that has enveloped me shall be broken, in the name of Jesus. The divine deposit of greatness in my life shall manifest by fire, in the name of Jesus. My God, the God of Abraham, Isaac and Jacob shall make the right people to help me at the right time and at the right place, in the name of Jesus. And beginning from now, God will turn my worst time to my best time, in the name of Jesus. Because of me, my family shall not know poverty again, in Jesus' name. Every environmental witchcraft that is flying against my greatness shall die, in the name of Jesus. I shall not struggle to be recognized, my God shall announce me, in the name of Jesus. The sun of my life shall not listen to the voice of the enemy; it shall arise and shine, in the name of Jesus. My destiny shall command my circumstances, in Jesus' name. The power of God shall single me out for honour, in Jesus' name. The power of God that has no respect for problems shall swallow my problems, in Jesus' name. Every agenda of darkness against my greatness shall be broken now, in Jesus' name. Whether my enemy likes it or not, I shall laugh last, in the name of Jesus. Amen."

Pick a song of praise and sing it to the glory of the name of God.

To every man and woman, a measure of divine internal treasure is planted. But if a person is not careful, his internal treasure can lie dormant from the cradle to the grave.

WAKE UP YOUR INNER TREASURE

The life of man is like a mirror. It never gives you back more than what you put before it. If you frown at it, it frowns back at you; if you smile at it, it smiles at you. The real tragedy in life is not when the life terminates but when it fails to fulfill God's purpose for it. It is a tragedy for somebody to have a talent and fail to use it until he dies. Life is also a one-way street. We cannot come back once we go through it. The problem is that a lot of people get wise when it is too late. The life you and I are living now is just like a loan from heaven. We are given the loan to trade here on earth. So, we are doing spiritual business for the Almighty with our lives.

Unfortunately, by the nature of human beings, many are at their best only when they are shaken and troubled. Many would not live well until they discover who they are. That is why life itself is a mystery and a mission. There is nothing more tragic than for a person to forfeit the reason why God has brought him to the world.

So, God has brought you to the world for a specific purpose. Each person is born to be remarkable. There are no two persons in the world that are exactly the same. It has been found that even identical twins are different. Your genetic make-up is for you alone. Your fingerprint is for you alone. Likewise, your life here is unique because God has a hand in it before the foundation of the world. That is why it is not good to come to the world and just mess around.

You must know what you are doing. The worst tragedy of life is what dies inside a man whilst he is still living. If one's life does not make an impact on others, it is a useless life. So, every man or woman is an unexplored gold mine. For God to send you to the world, He has planted something in you to make you great. The greatest discovery you can therefore make in life is to discover your God-given deposits or treasures. It is a day of tragedy if you allow the enemy to kill the treasures God has planted in you.

DIAMOND MINE OF GOLCONDA

A certain man owned and was living on a vast land. One day, a wise old priest visited him and asked him if he had diamond and he said, "No, I have never seen one before." The old priest said to him, "If you have a little bit of diamond, you will be so rich and you will have no problem." The man said, "Where can I find it?" The priest answered, "You should start looking for it where you find the river passing through two mountains. Check in the white sand very well and you will find diamond there." The man could no longer sleep and because of this urge within him to find diamond, he sold off his property and began to travel from place to place, looking for the river with white sand. He searched and searched until one day, he got fed up and jumped into a river and committed suicide. One month after he died, the fellow who bought his compound found a shiny object in the compound and took it. He put it on the table and sat down to look at it very well because he did not know what it was. The same wise old priest came again, and immediately he entered and saw this shining material on the table, he said, "Mr. Man, what is this?" He said, "I found it outside, in my garden." The old wise man said, "But this is diamond. The person who had this place sold it out to look for diamond and that was why he died. This is diamond." They did a test and the substance was confirmed to be diamond. By the time they started digging round that compound, it was discovered that the place had the largest deposit of diamond in the whole world. It was the diamond mine of Golconda. Here was a man who was living right on top of diamond but out of ignorance, he sold off the land and died a terrible death. What he was looking for that caused his death was in the land.

Perhaps you learnt carpentry or bricklaying; or you were in business and later became a civil servant, and later, you turned to another occupation, but in all, you did not make any progress, then something is wrong. Unto every man a measure of divine treasure has been granted. The Bible calls it hidden treasure. And just like precious metals in the physical world, spiritual treasures lie hidden from human beings. You do not get gold or oil on the surface of the earth. You go deep down to get them. Going deep down is where the problem lies. Many people in our today's world are surface people. They never really go down in their lives to see what has been deposited there and bring them out for the glory of God and for their own benefit. Incidentally, the children of darkness can see these things, and when they look at some believers, they shake their heads in pity.

One day, at Oyingbo market in Lagos, a woman wanted to buy meat but did not have the money to purchase it. She then asked for bones and started haggling over the bones. One of the demonic people selling herbs around there, who was watching her, shook his head and said, "If this woman was what she was supposed to be, she was not even supposed to come to the market to buy anything. People ought to bring the things she needed to her at home. But look at her now, she is bargaining for bones."

To every man and woman, a measure of divine internal treasure is planted. But if a person is not careful, his internal treasure can lie dormant from the cradle to the grave. That is why the cemetery is a bad place; it is a place that swallows many visions and dreams. It is a place where many people's dreams have become nightmares.

THINGS THAT CAN AFFECT YOUR HIDDEN TREASURE

The internal treasure can be stolen. In 1994, a certain man wanted to be rich at all cost. A witch doctor told him that for him to make that kind of money, he needed to sleep with three virgin girls and bring their blood to him. So, the man went to a girls' hostel in one of our universities with his big Mercedes Benz car to look for three girls. He found seven that were ready to collect money and do whatever he wanted. Those girls were ready to sell the treasures planted in them.

A treasure can be sold, stolen, or transferred to another person. It can be barred, it can be caged and it can be killed. God showed Joseph his treasure at a young age. His treasure was that he was going to be a leader. When his brothers sold him off, the treasure that was already awake in him followed him to the prison. Immediately he got to there, they made him the head because of that anointing. When they took him from the prison to the house of Potiphar, he also became a leader there. And from there, they took him to the king's palace where he also became a leader. Everywhere he went, that anointing to be a leader was on him. But it could have been stolen if he cooperated with Potiphar's wife. It would have been taken away and today, we would not be reading about him in the Bible.

Many people need to cry bitterly to the Lord. The reason some people are below the ladder now may be because of some careless sex they had when they were small boys or girls.

Sometime ago, I prayed for some girls from a university and they told me that they wanted to confess their sins. I said, "What are they?" They said they would bring something to show me the following day. That day, they came with a small pot in which there was some liquid. I asked what the substance was. They said it was the sperm they collected from boys in the campus. "Man Of God, to be quite honest with you, these boys are finished." I said, "You mean there can be no repair?" They said, if there would be any repair, it would be made by a strong man of God. The treasures of these boys have been taken away. That of Joseph would have been stolen the way that of Samson was easily stolen.

THE SEVEN TREASURES IN THE LIFE OF JOHN THE BAPTIST

When the Lord told the father of John the Baptist that he was going to have him, He also told him the treasures of the baby.

Luke 1:14- 15 says, **"And thou shalt have joy and gladness** (that is, that John the Baptist would bring joy and gladness) **and many shall rejoice at his birth. For he shall be great in the sight of the Lord, and shall drink neither wine nor strong drink."**

It means that if he drank wine or strong drink, he would not be great before the Lord. The Lord quickly added this so that John would be great. Anyone who drinks beer or other alcoholic drinks is demoting himself or herself and rubbishing his or her virtues.

Verse 15 continues: **"And he shall be filled with the Holy Ghost, even from his mother's womb."**

It means that a person could also be filled with evil spirits from his mother's womb. Verse 16: **"And many of the children of Israel shall he turn to the Lord their God"** (meaning that he would have the power to convict and convert). Verse 17: **"And he shall go before him in the spirit and power of Elias** (meaning that he would be a terror to the kingdom of darkness) **to turn the hearts of the fathers to the children, and the disobedient to the wisdom of the just; to make ready a people prepared for the Lord."**

The seven treasures listed here were planted in the life of John the Baptist.

Many people have seven, ten, twenty or fifty treasures planted in them but they are operating only on one and are complaining that things are not moving. You need to deal with yourself the way that tax collector dealt with himself. The Bible says that he slapped himself on the chest and cried to the Lord. You need to talk to yourself, you need to address your destiny and say to it: "My destiny, do not sleep." You must wake up those things that have been planted in you by the Lord, which you are not using. You must challenge them to come up. One of the greatest things you can do for yourself is to pray to find out those hidden treasures. Perhaps, if you pray and find them out, some of your running about will stop because you will discover that some of the things you are running about for are right there within you. This is why you must pray the life-waking up prayer points at the end of this book.

Many destinies and virtues are at various levels of slumber and some virtues have fallen into coma. They need an iron hand to shake them loose and bring them up. That iron hand is the prayer in this book, which should not be said casually, because it will not help only you but will also help those around you.

One day, a farmer went to the market and bought a rat trap. When he returned home and was bringing it out, Mr. Rat saw it from an opening in a wall. He became very sad because he knew that, soon, he would be unable to run about as freely as he would want to do. He went to Mr. Cock who was also in the yard and said to him: "Mr. Cock, do you know that they have bought a rat trap?" The cock said, "Well, that is your business," and the rat went away dejected. He ran to Mr. Pig, who also lived in the garden, and said to him: "Mr. Pig, do you know that they have a bought rat trap?" The pig said, "No problem, I will be praying for you," and Mr. Pig also took the matter casually. Mr. Rat was still not happy. He ran to Mr. Cow, who was also in the garden, and said to him: "Mr. Cow, do you know that they have bought a rat trap?" The cow said, "Yes, you should grow up like me, so that the trap will not be able to catch you." Mr. Rat retired to his hole and cried. The farmer set the trap at night and there was a noise when the trap caught something. The farmer's wife went out to see what the trap had caught, but because the place was dark she did not know that the trap had caught a snake. As she put her hand down, the snake which was at the point of death and very angry struck her and she fainted immediately. She was rushed to the hospital. She began to run fever and in those days, the treatment for fever was chicken soup. So, immediately they took her back to the house, they quickly killed Mr. Cock to prepare soup for her. So, Mr. Cock that did not give a damn when the rat trap was bought was the first casualty. The woman did not get well on time and people began to come to their house to greet her and because of the large number of visitors, Mr. Pig was slaughtered to prepare snacks to entertain the visitors. Again, Mr. Pig, who took the issue of the rat trap casually, became a casualty. To take the accompanying prayer points in this book casually can make you a casualty. Therefore, be wise.

I thank God for your life and for whatever job you are doing now. But do you know that, that ability could be just one over 50 of what God has deposited in you? You need to pray to wake up your inner treasure.

Unfortunately, many people are in a profession not because they like to be there but because their parents say they must be there.

SIGNS TO KNOW YOUR INTERNAL TREASURES

There are some signs and marks by which you may know your internal treasures:

1. Those things you are happy doing: Your treasure may be tied to the things you feel very happy doing. Many people may wake up on Monday mornings and go to the work they hate to do.

2. Those things in your life that can help others.

3. Those things in your life that are in high demand.

4. Those things that you can accomplish with minimal assistance. When I was a small boy, I had a friend called Ahmed. Anytime anything electrical went wrong, Ahmed could repair it, yet he had not even concluded his primary school education nor did he know the definition of physics, chemistry or biology. Unfortunately, his mother was one of those who took their children from one prophet to another. And one prophet told them that Ahmed was destined to be an accountant. Ahmed ended up in prison for

stealing as an accountant.

5. Those good desires that will not release you.

6. Those things that motivate you to be productive.

7. Those things in you which ignite in you the zeal to perform them.

8. Those difficult things that you do effortlessly.

9. Those things that you do which get positive response from others.

10. Those things that you do which cause doors to be opened to you with ease.

11. Those things that you do which give you a sense of personal satisfaction.

Unfortunately, many people are in a profession not because they like to be there but because their parents say they must be there. For example, they said you must be a doctor and you became one. They brought the first patient and he died. They brought the second patient and he died, and also the third patient. Everybody in the street gathered and told other patients: "If you do not want to die, do not go to that hospital. People who walked in there with their legs were carried out dead." I have a doctor friend like that. He is now into poultry business and has abandoned medical practice.

12. Those things you do which make you to develop new ideas.

13. Those things you do that make you think creatively.

14. Those things that make your spiritual leaders happy.

15. Those things that you are willing to pursue at any cost.

Many people were forced to learn carpentry or motor mechanic simply because they were failing their examinations in the school. They have learnt the trade but their brains remain the same. They are busy spoiling people's cars, and are not happy doing the work. There are many people working in frustration.

Sometime ago, I passed by a school and saw a teacher, who ran mad with his students. He beat them up so much and the whole class was crying. The teacher simply showed a mark of frustration.

16. Those things for which you will be willing to make a sacrifice.

17. The work you are doing for which you will feel confident to face God.

18. Those things you are doing about which God will say to you, "Well done."

19. Those things that the Lord has been bombarding your dreams with, which you

always see yourself doing.

20. Those things that you do which multiply your value, bring honour to you, and make people to glorify your God.

Apart from praying to the Holy Spirit to reveal to you your hidden treasure, you can locate them through these signs.

Where I attended my junior school, there used to be a madman in the nearby market called, "Lion of Judah." If we were not small boys, we would have known from that name that he had a problem. Otherwise, how would a man call himself the Lion of Judah? However, anytime we were taught mathematics in the school and we did not understand, all we needed do was to go to Lion of Judah in the market and say, "Lion of Judah, we were taught mathematics today and we do not understand it." His madness would stop temporarily and he would say, "Is it trigonometry, algebra or geometry?" When we told him, he would sit down and with his fingers in the sand, explain it to us the way that would make our teacher look stupid. If you say, "Lion of Judah, we were taught history today and I do not understand it." He would say, "Which aspect of history? Is it European history, World history or African history?" By the time you mentioned which one, he would give you a lecture that would look as if your teacher never went to school. When he concluded teaching, he would bring out his mouth organ and play it with both his mouth and nostrils.

It was from this mad man that I first of all heard these two strange words: Jewinization and Arabization. He did not talk about Christianity or Islam. Instead of talking of Christianity, he would say Jewinization of Africa and instead of Islam, he would say Arabization of Africa. But after his lecture, if you gave 'Lion of Judah' a bowl of rice, he would first of all pour it on the sand, lick the soup at the bottom of the pot or plate and then pack the sand and rice back into his plate and begin to eat it. I have no doubt in my mind that he was meant to be one of the greatest professors in the country but the enemy reduced him to nothing.

When something has been buried in a person's life right from the womb and he wants to take it away, he has to be violent. Remember that when Jesus got to the grave of Lazarus, He turned to His Father with a gentle voice and said, "Father I thank You because You always hear my prayers." But immediately He turned away from His Father to the grave, the gentleman in Him disappeared. He now roared, "Lazarus, come forth." You should therefore shout the following prayer points loud and clear:

PRAYER POINTS

1. Every hidden root problem, die, in the name of Jesus.
2. Every dark power hired against my greatness from my root, die, in the name of Jesus.
3. Blood of Jesus, break every demon of darkness assigned against my life, in the name of Jesus.
4. Every dark power operating in my root, your

time is up, die, in Jesus' name.

5. Every altar of darkness swallowing my greatness, scatter, in the name of Jesus.
6. My Father, plug me into your socket of breakthroughs, in Jesus' name.
7. My Father, my case shall receive the touch of heaven today, in Jesus' name.
8. Every power aborting the plan of God for my life, die, in the name of Jesus.
9. Treasures of my life, wake up by fire, in the name of Jesus.
10. Household witchcraft will not waste my life, in the name of Jesus.
11. I shall not live in shame; I shall not die in shame, in name of Jesus.
12. I shall not destroy the pages of my life, in the name of Jesus.
13. Every satanic finger pointed at my destiny, wither, in the name of Jesus.
14. My Pharaoh, I kill you today, in the name of Jesus.

15. If I be a child of God, let fire fall, in the name of Jesus.
16. Anything programmed into the heavenlies against my destiny, fall down and die, in the name of Jesus.
17. My Father, convert all my fears to ashes, in the name of Jesus.
18. Any power of profitless venture, die, in the name of Jesus.
19. Every desert power attacking my destiny, die, in the name of Jesus.
20. Oh net of my destiny, catch fishes in the ocean of life, in the name of Jesus.
21. Every demoting power in my family line, die, in the name of Jesus.
22. The enemy will not measure my length on the ground, in the name of Jesus.
23. The enemy will not convert my meat to bone, in the name of Jesus.
24. Authority of ease to possess my possession, come upon my life, in the name of Jesus.

Brokenness is the
opposite of arrogance
and pride and there
can be no meeting
point between a holy
God and a proud
person.
The man with the
broken heart is God's
best friend.

THE WAY UP IS DOWN

John 12: 24 says, "Verily, verily, I say unto you, Except a corn of wheat fall into the ground and die, it abideth alone: but if it die, it bringeth much fruit."

This verse is simply telling us that the way up is down. Spiritual experience is not magic and there is nobody that God cannot use. God does not have a problem with using people, the problem is availability. There are many people but only a few make themselves available. The scarcity of the power of God in any generation is not the fault of God but the unavailability of useable men and women.

It is a fantastic process of self-humiliation for Jesus our Lord and Saviour to come to us as a baby. When He was born, they had to take Him into hiding because of a mere man called Herod. That is a fantastic process of self-humility.

There are many soldiers in the house of God but the

problem is that some want to become Generals without first becoming captains. This verse is telling us that if we want to go far with God, the way to it is humility. The human heart is useless to God until it is broken. The human heart, no matter how intelligent or analytic it is, can be useless until the hammer of God presses it and breaks it into pieces. Psalm 34: 18 tells is about those the Lord is close to. It says, "**The Lord is nigh unto them that are of a broken heart; and saveth such as be of a contrite spirit.**

It did not say, to pastors or senior apostles.

BENEFITS OF BROKENNESS

Brokenness is an essential condition for God's presence in your life. It leads to greatness. So, if you want God to be close to you then He must break you. The Lord is near unto those that are of a broken heart. The reverse is also true. The Lord is far from the unbroken ones. That was what happened to the prodigal child in the Bible. He got broken, put shame aside and said, "I must arise and go to my father." He said, "Father, I have sinned before you, make me one of your servants, forget that I am one of your children." He was completely broken and he received mercy. The tax collector also in the Bible was broken. He said, "Lord, have mercy on me. I am a sinner." And the Bible says he went home justified.

A broken man may look like a fool sometimes but when the time comes, it would be clear who the fools are. So, if you want to rise up in God, the way is down.
Psalm 51: 17 says, **"The sacrifices of God are a broken spirit, a broken and contrite heart, O God thou will not despise."**

It means that there are some people that God despises. They may dress neatly, and may look sanctimonious, they may even be very good at calling prayer points and jumping up, but God despises them. If you say, "Well, if God refuses to use me, I will use myself." That would lead you nowhere.

Brokenness is the opposite of arrogance and pride and there can be no meeting point between a holy God and a proud person. The man with the broken heart is God's best friend. Peter was a broken man that was why God could use him. It is true that he made many mistakes but he was humble. When he betrayed Jesus contrary to his expectation, he went out and wept bitterly. He was a broken man. Anytime he was corrected, he quickly accepted the correction. Therefore, God was able to use him. God did not use him because he was better than the other apostles.

Sin came into the world through a proud spirit. Lucifer wanted to exalt himself higher than God. There is no short cut. If Jesus must increase in your life, you must decrease. The more of you in your life, the less of Jesus you will have.

Isaiah 57: 15 says, "**For thus saith the high and lofty one that inhabiteth eternity whose name is Holy, I dwell in the high and holy place with him also that**

is of contrite and humble spirit (so it means that the habitation of God is in two places. As high and exalted as God is, He abides in the heart of humble and broken men, and also in holy places) **to revive the spirit of the humble, and to revive the heart of the contrite ones."**

It means that you will not have spiritual revival in your life until you meet God in brokenness. God revives the humble and brokenhearted. So, for you to have spiritual revival in your life, brokenness is an essential element. It is good for you to know this now because the children of the devil are increasing their technics and strategies everyday. They are doing new research in order to track down Christians. You cannot afford to say you want to rely on the power of yesterday, or the power of last year. You must not sit down and start boasting that you were sanctified 25 years ago, therefore you do not need fire. They will swallow you and your sanctification. And if you are not careful, they will even swallow more things.

The present-day enemies have settled down to study every technic. They have swallowed all the traditional prayers people used to pray in the past. Most of those prayers do not make sense to those who are saying them. So, we need to move up, we need to be able to stand up and challenge all these negative powers that are speaking against our God. We need to wear the prophetic anointing, so that everywhere we are, we can take a decision for God. Even the way things are going now, no one can afford to be low in the spirit. We need to know when to go somewhere and when not to go. We need to know where to eat and where not to eat. You need to know the kind of place you follow people to. Life is becoming more dangerous and risky and the children of satan are increasing everyday. Now that they know that those who put their legs on the wall can easily be identified as witches, they do not operate that way anymore. Only a few of them are still doing so. They have changed their strategy but you are still claiming your sanctification of ten years ago. You need to move from that low level anointing. You need to understand how power comes upon people.

Many people cry for power but when God looks down from heaven and sees that they are not broken, He will not grant their request. No matter how much a father loves his four-year-old son, he will not give him a razor blade because he will cut himself. It is the same way God is looking at many people. You cannot want power with anger and unforgiving attitude still in your life. God will not give it to you because you will use it to destroy others. The Bible says that our generation is looking for the manifestation of the sons of God, it has not seen them. Instead what we have now are lots of commercial prophets and those who want to convert the house of God to a place of merchandise. Let the sons of God manifest.

Brokenness is to surrender. To surrender means to be willing to function within the area where God has called you; the willingness to fulfill God's purpose for your life. To surrender may not be very kind, but we have to do it. To surrender is to say, “Well, this is what God wants me to do and I must do it.” To surrender is the willingness to do God’s design for your life whether it is marriage, family or church. Many brothers and sisters are looking for sophisticated people to marry instead of looking for those who will favour their lives. When you surrender, you will follow what God wants you to do.

To surrender means to willingly submit to the authorities that God has placed over you. When you are broken, there would no longer be any resistance or rebellion to the work of God in your life. You will not be part of those who are a problem to the house of God. You will be one of those who will make the place to move forward. You will not be part of the problem; you will be part of the solution. To surrender is to totally yield yourself to the will and control of God. You will die to your opinions, preferences and tastes.

Many years ago, a certain sister came to the church for

service and was complaining bitterly. She said, "I don't know why I should come to a place like this. If not for the problem I have why should I come and sit here. I know my class." But the "Goliath" pursuing her did not recognize the class. You must die to your taste, will and the world. What excites the people of the world must not excite you. What they call enjoyment is not your own definition of enjoyment. People of the world think enjoyment is partying, smoking, and dancing their lives away. Their enjoyment is to put smoke and alcohol in the temple of God, which is their body. They lack understanding. When you surrender, you die to the world completely. You die to everything they do, you die to their approval. You die to their blame and you die to self. That is the meaning of the way up is down.

A man who is crucified with Christ has no right to self-pity, bitterness and retaliation. He is dead. Dead men have no right. Dead men have no place for fighting. If you can still get angry up to the level that somebody has to still hold you to prevent you from fighting, you are on your way to hell. You need to restructure your life until that thing in you that rises in anger dies then you are ready. Dead men do not complain, they do not gossip. Dead men do not fornicate, they do not backbite. They do not even hold grudges. They do not steal neither do they practise hypocrisy because they are dead completely and none of these things affect them.

Lack of brokenness makes people to be boastful. Many people in the house of God need to go back to the altar of God for a complete circumcision of the heart. Many people do not know anything about heaven yet. When they catch a glimpse of it, they would be humbled by force. When they see a little bit of hell fire too, they would sit up. It is good for people to be taken to the two places so that they can compare and contrast and choose which one they want to go out of the two places.

Brokenness is to see how your sin is. When pride comes into a person's life, the sins of other people will bother him more than his own sins. Proud people are not willing to admit that they are proud. Brokenness will change a self-righteous critical spirit to a humble soul. When you are at the centre of your life, you are not broken. You are far from the power of God. Immediately you achieve brokenness in your life, the power of God becomes automatic. Pampering lust instead of doing something about it will put you in trouble. The broken man would flee all appearances of evil.

Brokenness is allowing your will to be broken. When your will is broken, your actions would be led by the Holy Spirit. Just like the broken pot can hold no water, a broken life cannot hold pride. You need to call your own sins by the name God calls them. It is not enough to accept your sin; you must repent and begin to obey God.

It is much easier to be a Christian in church than at home. If you are looking for Christian men and women, do not go to the church, go to their homes. The way you live at home shows who is in control of your life. Only a mad person will slap his wife in the church. But at home, anything can happen.

Brokenness will change the way we receive rebuke or criticism. Seeds contain the potential of fruitfulness.

Seeds can never bring forth fruit until they enter the ground and are broken, and then the new plant can sprout. All farmers know that life comes out of death. The brokenness of a seed brings about a new life. You have to be completely broken before God for the door of blessings to be opened to you. No matter the trials facing you, when you are broken, know that there is a way out. Many who claim to be humble in the house of God are not. They have only been humbled by the enemy. This is not an emotional thing. It is an attitude of life. The choice is yours. If you fall afresh upon the

Cornerstone, you will be broken and will be blessed. And if you wait for the Cornerstone to fall upon you, it will smash you to pieces. It is only through brokenness that our lives can become acceptable to God and used for the kingdom purpose.

Brokenness is that sorrow and weeping for your sins. God does not have respect for people who are always going back to their sins. Brokenness is more than a crying spirit. In fact, many people cry but the cry does not come from within. But when you are truly broken, there is a power that comes into your life because brokenness has to do with the walls inside your soul. The power of God scatters those walls when you are broken and is able to move into your life.

THE UNBROKEN

People who are not broken are the ones always fellowshipping with evil people. They blend easily with them. When they see Christians, they would say, "Praise the Lord, glory be to the name of the Lord," they blend with them.

Unbroken people are blinded by working success. They respect people because of their wealth. Unbroken people live empty spiritual lives. The messages on holiness do not change them. They refuse to throw away their Jezebelian materials. They always go back to these materials after deliverance.

Unbroken people lack intimate relationship with Christ. They are prayer failures, Bible failures, selfish and proud. They lack knowledge and understanding, and are always backsliding. But broken people are always ready to pursue peace. They may be insulted or wronged but they do not act against anybody. When a broken person remembers how Jesus suffered, he or she would not fight as others fight him or her. Broken men honour others better than themselves. A broken person is dead to public opinion. Sometimes, the problem is that a lot of people believe that they know too much. They have read too many books and listened to too many experts and have forgotten the fundamental simple things. They have forgotten that when Jesus was on earth, the Scribes and the Pharisees did not receive blessings but the poor did. The Bible makes us to understand that wherever Jesus was accepted, the people were blessed. Many people followed Jesus but received nothing. Unbroken people want to become VIPs on earth. But the only way to become a VIP is to be broken.

A certain man prayed three powerful prayer points, which everyone needs to pray.

The first one was: "Oh Lord, save me from myself."
The second one was: "Oh Lord, let me be lost in thee."
And the third one was: "Oh Lord, let self die and let Christ live."

He started praying these prayers and became one of the greatest men of God that ever lived.

There is need for you to examine yourself and identify the stubborn areas which the Holy Spirit has not touched. It is quite unfortunate that men who are supposed to be running after the things of God and holiness are busy running after money. Many people do not understand that their greatest enemy is not the devil but themselves. That is why the following prayer point is expedient: "Oh Lord, show me the secret of my life, in Jesus' name." The greatest enemy of man is man himself because man makes himself available to the devil and he uses him. Examine yourself.

PRAYER POINTS

1. I will not come to the world in vain, in the name of Jesus.
2. Anything quenching the fire of God in my life, die, in the name of Jesus.
3. Oh God, take control of my dream life, in the name of Jesus.
4. Oh Lord, let my mind be lost in thee, in the name of Jesus.

5. Every stubborn stone in my soul, break, in the name of Jesus.
6. Every power blinding my vision, die, in the name of Jesus.
7. Every satanic door in my destiny, blood of Jesus, close it, in the name of Jesus.
8. Whatsoever needs to be done to promote my life, Oh Lord, do it, in the name of Jesus.
9. You my destiny, rise up by fire, in the name of Jesus.
10. Oh star of my destiny, arise and shine, in the name of Jesus.
11. Every cage of limitation in my family line, die, in the name of Jesus.
12. Thou power of the flesh in my life, die and receive the life of Christ, in the name of Jesus.
13. Oh God, arise and let me experience your transforming power, in the name of Jesus.

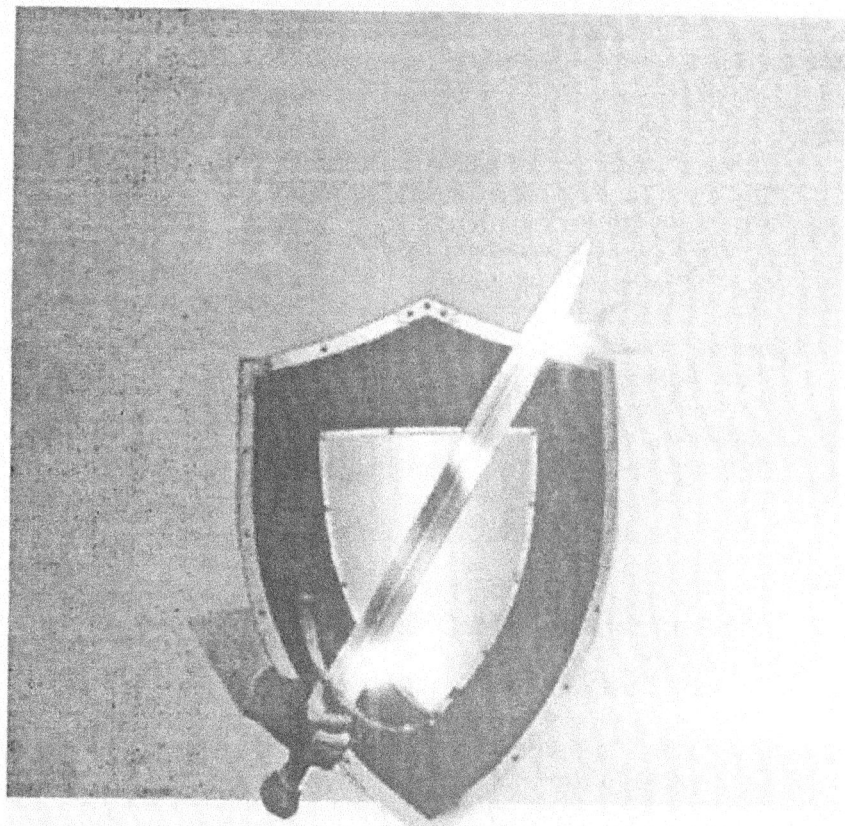

Other Publications

by

Dr. D.K. Olukoya

1. 20 Marching Order To Fulfill Your Destiny
2. 30 Things The Anointing Can Do For You
3. 30 Poverty Destroying Keys
4. 30 Prophetic Arrows From Heaven
5. A-Z Of Complete Deliverance
6. Abraham's Children In Bondage
7. Basic Prayer Patterns
8. Battle Against the Wasters
9. Be Prepared
10. Bewitchment Must Die
11. Biblical Principles Of Dream Interpretation
12. Biblical Principles Of Long Life
13. Born Great, But Tied Down
14. Breaking Bad Habits
15. Breakthrough Prayers For Business Professionals
16. Bringing Down The Power Of God
17. Brokenness
18. Can God Trust You
19. Can God?
20. Command The Morning
21. Connecting To The God Of Breakthroughs
22. Consecration Commitment & Loyalty
23. Contending For The Kingdom
24. Criminals In The House Of God
25. Dancers At The Gate Of Hell
26. Dealing With The Evil Powers Of Your Father's House
27. Dealing With Tropical Demons
28. Dealing With Local Satanic Technology
29. Dealing With Witchcraft Barbers
30. Dealing With Unprofitable Roofs
31. Dealing With Hidden Curses
32. Dealing With Destiny Vultures
33. Dealing With Satanic Exchange
34. Dealing With Destiny Thieves
35. Deliverance Of The Head
36. Deliverance Of The Tongue

37. Deliverance : God's Medicine Bottle
38. Deliverance From Evil Load
39. Deliverance From Spirit Husband And Spirit Wife
40. Deliverance From The Limiting Power
41. Deliverance From Evil Foundation
42. Deliverance Of The Brain
43. Deliverance Of The Conscience
44. Deliverance By Fire
45. Destiny Clinic
46. Destroying Satanic Marks
47. Disgracing Soul Hunters
48. Divine Yellow Card
49. Divine Prescription For Your Totally Immunity
50. Divine Military Training
51. Dominion Prosperity
52. Drawers Of Powers From The Heavenlies
53. Evil Appetite
54. Evil Umbrella
55. Facing Both Ways
56. Failure In The School Of Prayer
57. Fire For Life's Journey
58. Fire For Spiritual Battles For The 21st Century Army
59. For We Wrestle...
60. Freedom Indeed
61. Fresh Fire(Bilingual Book In French)
62. God's Key To A Happy Home
63. Healing Through Prayers
64. Holiness Unto The Lord
65. Holy Fever
66. Holy Cry
67. Hour Of Decision
68. How To Obtain Personal Deliverance
69. How To Pray When Surrounded By The Enemies
70. I Am Moving Forward
71. Idol Of The Heart
72. Igniting Your Inner Fire

73. Igniting Your Inner Fire
74. Is This What They Die For
75. Killing Your Goliath By Fire
76. Killing The Serpent Of Frustration
77. Let God Answer By Fire
78. Let Fire Fall
79. Limiting God
80. Looking Unto Jesus
81. Lord, Behold Their Threatening
82. Madness Of The Heart
83. Making Your Way Through The Traffic Jam Of Life
84. Meat For Champions
85. Medicine For Winners
86. By Burden For The Church
87. Open Heaven Through The Disturbance
88. Overpowering Witchcraft
89. Passing Through The Valley Of The Shadow Of Death
90. Paralysing The Riders And The Horse
91. Personal Spiritual Check-Up
92. Possessing The Tongue Of Fire
93. Power To Recover Your Birthright
94. Power Against Captivity
95. Power Against Coffin Spirits
96. Power Against Unclean Spirits
97. Power Against The Mystery Of Wickedness
98. Power Against Destiny Quenchers
99. Power Against Dream Criminals
100. Power Against Local Wickedness
101. Power Against Marine Spirits
102. Power Against Spiritual Terrorists
103. Power To Recover Your Lost Glory
104. Power To Disgrace The Oppressor
105. Power Must Change Hands
106. Power Must Change Hands (Prayer Points From 1995-2010
107. Power To Shut Satanic Doors
108. Power Against The Mystery Of Wickedness

109. Power Of Brokenness
110. Pray Your Way To Breakthroughs
111. Prayer To Make You Fulfill Your Divine Destiny
112. Prayer Strategies For Spinsters And Bachelors
113. Prayer Warfare Against 70 Mad Spirit
114. Prayer Is The Battle
115. Prayer To Kill Enchantment
116. Prayer Rain
117. Prayer To Destroy Diseases And Infirmities
118. Prayer For Open Heavens
119. Prayers To Move From Minimum To Maximum
120. Praying Against Foundational Poverty
121. Praying Against The Spirit Of The Valley
122. Praying In The Storm
123. Praying To Dismantle Witchcraft
124. Praying To Destroy Satanic Roadblocks
125. Principles Of Conclusive Prayers
126. Principles Of Prayer
127. Raiding The House Of The Strongman
128. Release From Destructive Covenant
129. Revoking Evil Decrees
130. Safeguarding Your Home
131. Satanic Diversion Of The Black Race
132. Secrets Of Spiritual Growth & Maturity
133. Self-Made Problems (Bilingual Book In French)
134. Seventy Rules Of Spiritual Warfare
135. Seventy Sermons To Preach To Your Destiny
136. Silencing The Birds Of Darkness
137. Slave Masters
138. Slaves Who Love Their Chains
139. Smite The Enemy And He Will Flee
140. Speaking Destruction Unto The Dark Rivers
141. Spiritual Education
142. Spiritual Growth And Maturity
143. Spiritual Warfare And The Home
144. Stop Them Before They Stop You

145. Strategic Praying
146. Strategy Of Warfare Praying
147. Students In The School Of Fear
148. Symptoms Of Witchcraft Attack
149. Taking The Battle To The Enemy's Gate
150. The Amazing Power Of Faith
151. The God Of Daniel (Bilingual Book In French)
152. The God Of Elijah (Bilingual Book In French)
153. The Vagabond Spirit
154. The Unlimited God
155. The Wealth Transfer Agenda
156. The Way Of Divine Encounter
157. The Unconquerable Power
158. The Baptism By Fire
159. The Battle Against The Spirit Of Impossibility
160. The Chain Breaker
161. The Dining Table Of Darkness
162. The Enemy Has Done This
163. The Evil Cry Of Your Family Idol
164. The Fire Of Revival
165. The School Of Tribulation
166. The Gateway To Spiritual Power
167. The Great Deliverance
168. The Internal Stumbling Block
169. The Lord Is A Man Of War
170. The Mystery Of The Mobile Curses
171. The Mystery Of The Mobile Temple
172. The Prayer Eagle
173. The University Of Champions
174. The Power Of Aggressive Prayer Warriors
175. The Power Of Priority
176. The Tongue Trap
177. The Terrible Agenda
178. The Scale Of The Almighty
179. The Hidden Viper
180. The Star In Your Sky

217. Your Mouth And Your Deliverance
218. Your Mouth And Your Warfare

YORUBA PUBLICATIONS

1. Adura Agbayori
2. Adura Ti Nsi Oke Ni Dii
3. Ojo Adura

FRENCH PUBLICATIONS

1. Pluie De Prière
2. Esprit De Vagabondage
3. En Finir Avec Les Forces Maléfiques De La Maison De Ton Père
4. Que L'envoutement Périsse
5. Frappez L'adversaire et il Fuira
6. Comment Recevoir La Deliverance Du Mari Et De La Femme De Nuit
7. Comment Se Délivrer Soi–meme
8. Pouvoir Contre Les Terroristes Spirituels
9. Prière De Percées Pour Les Homes D'affaires
10. Prier Jusqu'a Remporter La Victoire
11. Prières Violentes Pour Humilier Les Problèmes Opiniâtres
12. Prière Pour Détruire Les Maladies Et Les Infirmités
13. Le Combat Spiritual Et Le Foyer
14. Bilan Spiritual Personnel
15. Victories Sur Les Rêves Sataniques
16. Priers De Combat Contre 70 Esprits Déchaînés
17. La Deviation Satanique De La Race Noire
18. Ton Combat Et Ta Stratégie
19. Votre Fondement Et Votre Destin
20. Révoquer Les Décrets Maléfiques
21. Cantique Des Cantiques
22. Le Mauvais Cri Des Idoles
23. Quand Les Choses Deviennent Difficiles
24. Les Strategies De Priers Pour Les Célibataires

25. Se Libérer Des Alliances Maléfiques
26. Démanteler La Sorcellerie
27. La Deliverance: Le Flacon De Medicament De Dieu
28. La Deliverance De La Tête
29. Commander Le Matin
30. Ne Grand Mais Lie
31. Pouvoir Contre Les Demons Tropicaux
32. Le Programme De Transfert Des Richesse
33. Les Etudiants A L'école De La Peur
34. L'étoile Dans Votre Ciel
35. Les Saisons De La Vie
36. Femme Tu Es Libérée

ANNUAL 70 DAYS PRAYER AND FASTING PUBLICATIONS

1. Prayers That Bring Miracles
2. Let God Answer By Fire
3. Prayers To Mount With Wings As Eagles
4. Prayers That Bring Explosive Increase
5. Prayers For Open Heavens
6. Prayers To You Fulfill Your Divine Destiny
7. Prayers That Make God To Answer And Fight By Fire
8. Prayers That Bring Unchallengeable Victory And Breakthrough Rainfall Bombardments
9. Prayers That Bring Dominion Prosperity And Uncommon Success
10. Prayers That Bring Power And Overflowing Progress
11. Prayers That Bring Laughter And Enlargement Breakthroughs
12. Prayers That Bring Uncommon Favour And Breakthroughs
13. Prayers That Bring Unprecedented Greatness & Unmatchable Increase
14. Prayers That Bring Awesome Testimonies And Turn Around Breakthroughs

ALL OBTAINABLE AT:

322, Herbert Macaulay Street,
2nd Floor, Old First Bank Building,
Sabo-Yaba, P.O.Box 12272,
Ikeja, Lagos.

MFM International Bookshop,
13, Olasimbo Street, Onike, Yaba, Lagos.

IPFY Music Konnections Limited,
48, Opebi Road, Salvation Bus Stop
(234-1-4719471,234-8033056093).

All MFM Church Branches Nationwide

www.ingramcontent.com/pod-product-compliance
Lightning Source LLC
Chambersburg PA
CBHW060953040426
42445CB00011B/1144
9780692388082